The True-or-False Book of
CATS

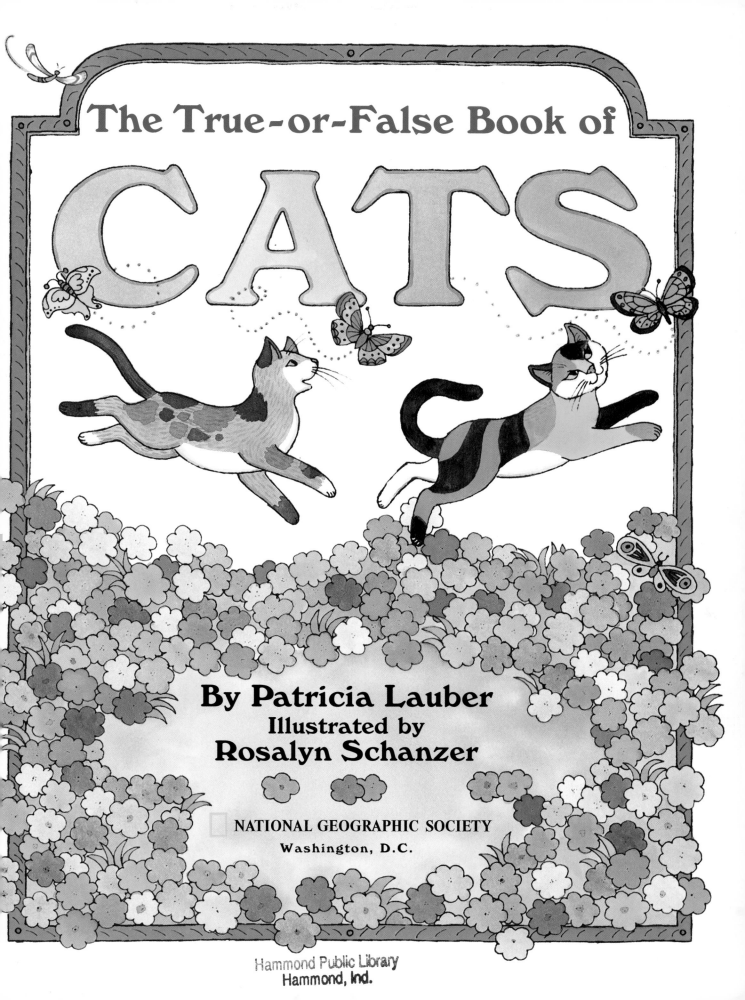

By Patricia Lauber
Illustrated by
Rosalyn Schanzer

NATIONAL GEOGRAPHIC SOCIETY
Washington, D.C.

This book is for Willie Thompson
Biggers & Small
Beemer and MeeToo.
P. L.

And for Spot.
R. S.

The author wishes to thank Dr. John Seidensticker, Curator of Mammals
at the National Zoological Park, Smithsonian Institution
and Kevin J. Craw, D.V. M., for their helpful comments.

Text copyright ©1998 Patricia Lauber
Illustrations copyright © 1998 Rosalyn Schanzer
Published by the National Geographic Society
1145 17th Street N.W.
Washington, D.C. 20036

Library of Congress Cataloging-in-Publication Data
Lauber, Patricia
The true-or-false book of cats / by Patricia Lauber ; illustrated by Rosalyn Schanzer.
p.   cm.
Summary: Discusses the truth behind such beliefs as "Cats can see in total darkness,"
"Cats have nine lives," and "A cat signals its feelings with its tail."
ISBN 0–7922–3440–5
1. Cats—Behavior—Miscellanea—Juvenile literature. [1. Cats—Miscellanea.]
I. Schanzer, Rosalyn, ill. II. Title.
SF445.7.L38 1998
636.8—dc21   97–11144   CIP
The Society is supported through membership dues and income
from the sale of its educational products.
Call 1–800-NGS-LINE for more information or
visit our website at nationalgeographic.com.

Printed in Hong Kong

CONTENTS

*

Cats and People

*

Thousands of years ago, some Old World peoples learned to plant seeds and grow crops. They harvested grain and stored it for later use. Soon they had a problem. Armies of field mice discovered the stores of grain. They moved in to feast on it.

In some areas, small wild cats discovered the armies of mice. They moved in to feast on the mice that were feasting on the grain. And that was how people and cats first came to know each other.

Cats were prized as mouse-catchers. Friendly ones were soon prized as pets.

Sailors and other travelers learned about these cats. They bought or stole cats and took them home. In this way, tame cats spread all over the Old World.

Later, the New World was discovered. Its settlers brought their cats. When pioneers moved west, they took their cats. Almost everywhere, cats were treasured as pets and as the world's best mousetraps.

Today's cats still catch mice. But they are mostly valued as pets, because they are affectionate, clean, quiet, and easy to care for.

See how much you know about cats. Read each statement in this book. Decide whether it's true or false. Then read the answer. Give yourself a score of Purrfect or Nearly Purrfect.

Cats don't like to be stared at.
*
True or false?

Watch two cats lock eyes and stare at each other. The staring is not friendly. Finally, one gives in and looks away. With luck, no fur will fly. To a cat, a stare is a threat. And so it is true that cats don't like to be stared at.

Your own cat likes to look at you, and it likes you to look back. But be sure to blink or to half-close your eyes.

Your cat may do the same. Looking without staring is like blowing kisses—it's warm and friendly.

Cats often sit in the laps of guests who don't like cats.
Some people think the cats are being mean, but they really aren't. When a cat enters a room, guests who like cats usually stare at the cat. A guest who doesn't like cats looks away. To the cat, this person seems the friendliest one in the room—with the best lap to sit in.

**A cat that rubs against your legs
is saying hello.**

*

True or false?

Rubbing is one way that cats greet people, and so it's true that the cat is saying hello. But the cat is also doing something else. It is marking you, and the mark says, "This person belongs to me."

Cats have special scent glands on their heads and tails. When a cat rubs against you, it rubs its scent on you. Humans can't smell this scent, which is probably just as well. But other cats can.

Cats have a keen sense of smell. They may spend minutes sniffing a person, a rug, or a place where some other animal has been. No one knows what they are learning, but it seems to be very interesting.

Cats can see in total darkness.
*
True or false?

If there is no light at all, no one can see. So it's false to say that cats can see in total darkness. But cats don't need much light to see. They can see when you can't. That's why it seems as if they can see without light.

In many ways, human eyes and cat eyes are alike. Light enters the eye through a hole called the pupil. It falls on an area behind the eyeball. This area is lined with millions of cells. They sense light and send messages to the brain. The brain makes sense out of the messages, and the person or cat sees.

A cat's eyes have extra cells that human eyes don't have. These cells act like mirrors. They gather up light that escaped the light-sensing cells. They bounce the light back into the eye. A cat uses every bit of light that enters its eyes. That is the main reason why it sees well in dim light.

Cats can't see color.

*

True or false?

Like human eyes, cat eyes have two kinds of cells that sense light. These are called rods and cones. Rods sense dim light, in which no color is seen. Cones sense bright light, in which color can be seen.

Even so, scientists long thought it was true that cats cannot see color. Cats are most active at night, when there is no color. In hunting, cats find their prey by sound and movement, not by color. So, these scientists said, cats don't need to see color—and cannot see color.

Today's scientists say that is false, that cats can see color. Cats do not pay much attention to color. But tests show that they can see it.

Many cat owners have long been sure their cats see color. A pet cat may, for example, always choose a pink ball instead of a blue, purple, or yellow one. It can also tell its own bowl by color.

A cat's whiskers are feelers.

*

True or false?

When people speak of a cat's whiskers, they usually mean the long whiskers on the upper lip. Look carefully and you will see many more. There are whiskers on the chin, over the eyes, and far back on the cheeks. There are also whiskers on the back of the front legs.

All these whiskers are feelers. In fact, they are remarkable feelers.

12

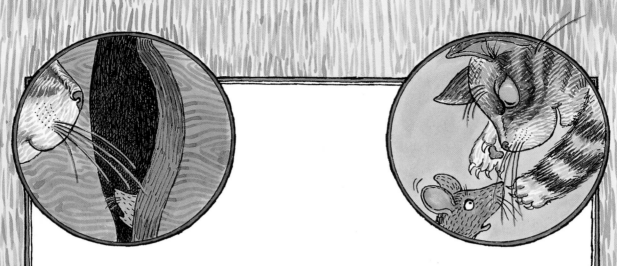

Whiskers help a cat judge if there is room for its body to squeeze through a small opening.

Lip whiskers are used in hunting. When a cat catches a mouse, its whiskers surround the prey. The cat senses the shape of the mouse and knows exactly where to bite.

Whiskers also help a cat move about in the dark. Although cats can see in the dark, they do not see as well as they do with more light. Whiskers give them extra information about what lies ahead.

The whiskers sense air currents. When air currents meet a rock or some other object, they change direction and go around the object. A cat's whiskers sense this tiny change. The cat learns that something is in its path. That is how whiskers work with eyesight and help a cat find its way in the dark.

Cats hear sounds that humans can't hear.

*

True or false?

Cats have sharp ears and can hear many things that people can't. They hear sounds that are too faint for human ears. They also hear sounds that are too high-pitched for human ears, such as the squeaks of mice.

When cats hunt, their eyes and ears work together. A cat holds still, waits, looks, and listens. A tiny rustle, a high-pitched squeal, or a moving leaf may tell of prey.

A cat's outer ears collect sounds. They are very good at this — they can be turned forward, sideways, or back. Each ear moves by itself. A cat can turn one forward and one back.

Watch a cat and you will see it is always listening. Even a napping cat is listening. If something interesting happens, the cat is up and awake in a flash.

Old cats, like old humans, do not hear high-pitched sounds as well as young ones.

**Cats can sense that an earthquake
is going to happen.**

*

True or false?

Time and again, people have reported that their cats became
very upset an hour or two before a big earthquake took place.
The cats suddenly rushed about the house, trying to get out.
Once out, they fled from buildings. Mother cats ran back and
forth, carrying their kittens out of the house.

Cats don't understand what an earthquake is. But it does
seem to be true that they sense something strange, and it
frightens them. Perhaps they hear sounds that people can't
hear. Perhaps they sense something else.

Scientists know that quakes are caused by forces inside the earth. The forces put strain on rock. When the rock snaps or shifts, an earthquake takes place. Before a quake, many small changes take place in the earth. Scientists have instruments that tell them about some of these changes. But they would like very much to know what it is that cats sense.

Cats need to sharpen their claws.
*
True or false?

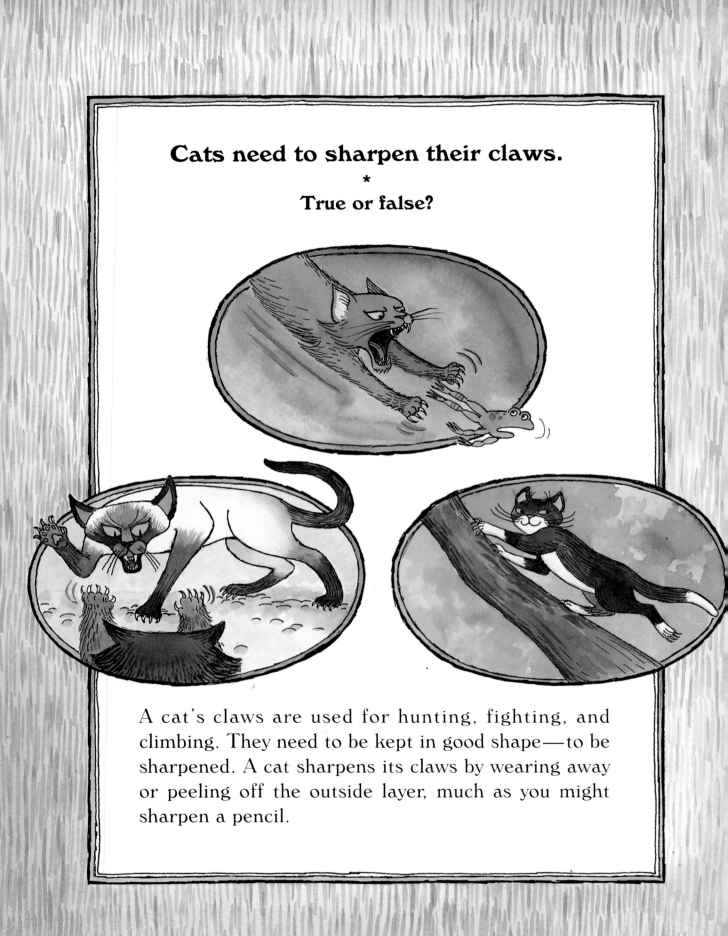

A cat's claws are used for hunting, fighting, and climbing. They need to be kept in good shape—to be sharpened. A cat sharpens its claws by wearing away or peeling off the outside layer, much as you might sharpen a pencil.

The front claws are curved needles. They can be moved in and out. Some of the time they are drawn in and hidden. Some of the time they are out and in use. A cat sharpens them on trees—and on rugs, furniture, and even scratching posts. You may find what looks like a claw in a place where a cat has been scratching. It's an outside layer that came off whole.

A cat having a good scratch is also getting some exercise. It is exercising its shoulder muscles and the muscles that move its front claws.

The hind claws cannot be drawn all the way in. They wear down as a cat walks or runs, and so they are blunter than the front claws. Cats keep these claws in shape by chewing off the outer layers.

20

Cats have a hard time coming down trees.

*

True or false?

Using its claws and its strong muscles, a cat can go up a tree as fast as it can run. The hind legs push. The curved front claws hook and grip the tree trunk. But coming down is not so easy. Most cats have a hard time. The muscles of the hind leg are most suited to pushing forward—and up.

A cat comes down rear first so that its claws will act as hooks. But the hind claws do not grip the tree well—the cat is really hanging by its front claws. To start down is to slide. To make matters worse, a cat has good eyesight. It can see that the ground is far away. A cat may spend hours in a tree, wailing for human help. Finally, it starts to slip and slide down. Once it nears the ground, the cat turns and jumps the rest of the way.

Cats have nine lives.

*

True or false?

Like other animals, and people, cats have one life, not nine. But cats may seem to have more than one life because they are quick and nimble. They often escape harm when another animal might not.

For example, cats are excellent climbers, but they do sometimes fall. In a flash, a falling cat rights itself, twisting its head and body. It stretches all four legs toward the ground and arches its back. All this happens too fast for the human eye to see. But slow-motion film shows how a falling cat is able to land on its feet.

Cats have dreams.

*

True or false?

Scientists have studied sleep in cats much as they have studied sleep in humans. They can tell which parts of the brain are active. They can tell if the eyes are moving—rapid eye movement is a sign of dreaming. And they say that cats do dream.

Cats sleep a lot, as much as 16 hours a day. Most of the time they are taking short naps—catnaps. They also settle down for longer sleeps. First there is a long, light sleep. Next there is a short, deep sleep. After that there is light sleep, then deep.

Cats dream when they are in deep sleep. If you are watching, you will see paws, tail, or whiskers twitch. The cat may growl, purr, or make other sounds. Probably it is dreaming of catching mice, sitting in a lap, eating a tasty meal, having a fight. But we will never know for sure.

Nobody really knows why cats bring home their prey.

*

True or false?

Mother cats bring mice to their kittens. They use the mice to teach the young how to hunt. Some people think that cats are trying to teach us to hunt by bringing home prey. But this does not seem likely. A cat simply puts its prey down and walks away. It does not show its person what to do with a mouse, a mole, a snake, a frog.

Perhaps the prey is a present. It is something the cat likes, and it is something you do not catch for yourself. But the truth is, nobody knows for sure why cats bring prey home.

A cat signals its feelings with its tail.

*

True or false?

You can tell how a cat is feeling by looking at its tail—that's true.

"I'm at peace with the world."

"I'm feeling friendly."

"I give up. Don't hurt me."

"Now you've done it. I'm really angry."

"I'm cross."

"I'm going to attack."

A cat's ears also signal its feelings.

*

True or false?

Like its tail, a cat's ears are clues to its feelings.

"I'm relaxed and at peace."

"What's that I hear?"

"I don't really want to fight, but I'll get my ears out of the way, just in case."

"I'm ready to attack."

"All's right with the world."

Purrs and meows are just noises that cats make.

*

True or false?

Cats cannot talk in words, but they have many ways of saying how they feel. Purrs and meows are much more than just noises.

Purring is a sign of friendliness—like a human smile, it says, "I mean you no harm." It is often a sign of a contented cat.

A gentle meow or a sound like "**brrp**," says, "Here I am. Hi!"

A louder meow demands attention, asking you to open a door or window or to fix the cat's dinner.

A different meow may mean that a cat is wet, lonely, lost, or in trouble ("Somebody has shut me in the closet!").

MEYOW!

YOOOW!

Screams and yowls tell of pain, mating, or a cat fight.

SSSSSSSSssss

A hiss says, "Watch out!"

When a cat sees prey it cannot reach, its teeth may chatter. The sound means, "I'd like to get my teeth in you."

CHATTER!

O solomeow!

Some scientists have taped the sounds that cats make. They say cats make a great variety of sounds, perhaps more than any other kind of animal. Listen carefully. You may be surprised at what you hear and learn.